DOWN WITH THE SHIP

DOWN WITH THE SHIP

Ryan Murphy

OTIS BOOKS/SEISMICITY EDITIONS
The Graduate Writing Program
Otis College of Art and Design
LOS ANGELES ● 2006

I would like to thank the editors of the journals in which some
of these poems first appeared: *Boog City, can we have our ball back,
The Canary, Chelsea, The Cortland Review, Court Green, The Denver
Quarterly, The Hat, The New Review of Literature, The Paris Review,*
and *Spinning Jenny.*

Some of these poems appeared in the chapbooks
On Violet Street (the Aldrich Museum of Contemporary Art),
Ocean Park (A Rest Press), *The Gales* (Pound for Pound Press)
and *Poems for Pitchers* (Sea. Lamb. Press.)

I would like to thank my parents, Nancy and Michael Murphy as
well as my sisters and brother, Sarah, Matthew and Caitlin.
Thank you Patrick Masterson and Paul Stephens.

Book design and typesetting: Yuko Sawamoto

OTIS BOOKS/SEISMICITY EDITIONS
The Graduate Writing Program
Otis College of Art and Design
9045 Lincoln Boulevard
Los Angeles, CA 90045

www.otis.edu
seismicity@otis.edu

For Kira

The Pursuit of Pleasure

I run some errands. The clouds
leaden bellies, all those white flowers
that started up around you.
We mourn the loss
of our nature poets.
However too much time alone is also lonely.
The trash won't take itself out you know.
When I am sweaty I like to lie
very still, all day Nintendo.
Did you fallow deciduous summer?
Today is the Post Office. Then
the pinecone of solitude.

A wave is not The Wave
when you're the only one standing.

Seven Stanzas

Vestibule sour summer clouds
Clasp sun June
Heliotrope's a mouth's morning
is a going out

Where quiet's not
through blinds wrings day
apple trees ardor bent
crucible or charming

Seen ends seeing composed and keeping
Look you are the urn
you are the spigot
O borealis marooned and clasp

Parsed and paling hussy
a lone a lost
cambric green dalliance
Come closer come on close your eyes

Daughter of drought
mourning white scythe each blossom
each blade
each spoke

The Comet's Tale

At the divinity school students
rehearse the Last Supper,
the Hare Krishnas have been evicted
from the East Village!
Traffic thunders up the night.

I've come to sing you a song called December.
How a slice of moon,
how a citrus sky.
The feeling going down.

Alka-Seltzer, auburn,
creosote, combine.
I resolve.

A radio plays the Yankees game
indistinctly. Hoarse and stitch, voice
to muzzle, muzzle
to snout.

Pleiades, (I'm tired)
go out, go out
shone their shadows.

The Matchbook Diaries

On a train, near winter.
Sickening in the glow.

So-and-so was here.
The both of us.

*

To step, each step –
to wile away.

*

Bright pavilions of gas stations.
Crocuses and touch-me-nots.

If locusts bend to their reflections.
If indigo.

*

Across the pivotal,
stilled a we –

And, out of nothing, a breathing.
The poor only words I know.

*

Hammerfull,
the sea thus.

The border from which
a heavier light depends.

*

The sidewalks flash silver with mica.
Skyline smeared with geese.

By way of recognition
I lost the sound of your voice.

*

Splint of blossoms and Blue
Heron. Sunlight rapid

on the rocks of a shallow stream.
Undoing and

*

Dear K,
I cannot write a sonnet.

The smell of tulips
doesn't remind me of anyone.

*

Blot of moon through the rush-grass.
The humid air a gray bride.

*

Consider how the shadows lean,
and despite insomnia

how the room outlasts you.
No single light.

The Lonely Bridge

They will never say,
come unglued,
like at night.

Headlights peeled like grapes.
Arbors, arms, etc.

What is was familiar.
What is like at night
familiar say what

The petunia has bent a little
over on its stem. Cold is
the current of the air.

"She's an architecture,"
 sing the wind-whisked cables,
"cold is the screws
 to hold my eyes."

Alloy Sun

Alloy sun.
The sun breaks on the rocks.
Sunkist™.

I sob in my black bean soup.
The rope that parts on the tilt of dark.
The sky fills with more

lovely and bankrupt
we abscond. Come off it.
In a moment we invent the dream
to explain our jerking awake.

Root system of stars,
the elms that open their umbrellas of night.
O September, O October, O November –
You can take this job and shove it.

Untitled

The sun's merely a spot
where the sun used to be.

Vague are the filament
sky. Stippled sky,
asphalt and water, sheesh.

Pale hands fold
themselves, like the Twin
Donut, into winter.

Seen from a train platform
a locust grows from the
wreck of an elevator winch.

I don't mean,
mean to say,
upset you.

Sometimes now the days
empty: the courtyard, the
courtyard, the doorjamb.

Beach leaves shuffle greens
and the tides go:
bitter, beacon, under.

Carriage

> *But never say that*
> *Beautifully you speak*
> — SAPPHO
> Translated by GUY DAVENPORT

The geese come warping in.
On pitched breath fall
forward, your stalled eyes –
these lampposts, mist-strewn

in Little Odessa, the sky gone russet,
gone squalor. It is morning
I have yet to recover: tracks of light
on the parquet,

what spring,
all shuttle-blown and cockscomb,
left restless, ungathered.

From a list of flowers:

gladiola
crocus
daffodil
verdant
honeysuckle
[   ]
cowslip

The Late Quartets

And the blind bird in the hibiscus
you could catch it in your hands
and its wings beat against the shell of your hands.

Many years after the accident at the well
the islanders are falling again to sleep,
gravel in her song.

Occasionally the traffic running parallel
the river
are similar.

And these momentary convergences
a catalogue of "still" and "no longer."
She wears a ring the color of his eyes.

Meanwhile the late quartets spill on directionless –
that night under the cherry tree and violet sky, etc.
Slowly it's become your New York again without you.

Dust pinwheels in a column of light,
fruit flies circling the sink.

whose one move discounts all possible others...

Sakura Park

Twilight emerging early and often now
more and more.
The aquarium of a room, the strips
of light on the ceiling illuminated
by a streetlight, listing trains as they shiver
through the blinds.

And the toilet is running,
and it's autumn all at once.

To describe how it felt, and not to know
the names of the trees outlining the park,
what to call the ordinary sunlight
sifting through the leaves.

So slow
I never knew
you took yourself away.

Morning and After

1
Bellwether clouds abject weather,
calves of winter. Riverbank machinations,
pigeons frozen on cornices, super-size my fries.

Six loads of laundry. Consensus
sums, virgin calendar. Apple
slices brown on the counter.

Yet aquarium-lit, the dull rush
of plumbing, the hum of your hard drive
signals effort around us.

2
Chorus to rut is forgetful
violence. I will wring your washcloth,
I will honor your coupon.

From my desk at the window
a green apple, the courtyard,
a small trapezoid of sky.

Shop talk, bride-to-be, housewife winters.
Lick jam from your fingers.
Beneath blight contend.

Number

You widow me
from pillar to post.
I scant, I gloss...

At the bottom
of the third the
Red Sox trail by two.

I want to play left
out, orange sherbet,
Schubert, Schubert, Schubert.

Complete mills from unrest:
routine breaks routine breaks,
what do you want

to say? pearlescent
atmosphere, thunderstorm
skyline, I like

to watch tv. At hour's end
tributaries unfettered
Hudson's gray like

But you, toward whom
nothing and everywhere
and just in time.

Untitled

It is what fills the space left
by the absence of your silhouette
in the doorway. It is somewhat
less than you may have hoped:

the imagination before its object
obliterates the pure orange dark.
A moan begins in the valley
like a truck in low gear.

Having returned here,
you find it less the world
you left than the one you expect:
what is only real cannot help

but describe its small arc
on the planet's surface.
The frogs gather their random chorus
into crowded song, the cat

drags a dead shrew into the light.
But be sure: there is
a sound before its voice
can be distinguished, a light

before its distance can be judged,
the startle of a shadow
before its gesture can be understood
as your own.

City of the Big Bang

A scope sun till unfurled
throat shaft
a drowned in shadow

willow camphor string
of colored lights around the yard

Of what are made the hopes
and fears of Kristy Yamaguchi?

First the wish for rain
in humidity
then rain and hail

damaging the blossoms
and fine cherry harvest
You're undressing in the dark

You're undressing in the shotgun light
of a Coors can
What tides await us

Sincerely, Hokusai

Dear Roger Clemens

New York is not eternity,
it is a monument.

I have not written a word in weeks. I keep thinking
of rooms in the bright houses
of Guadalajara. I am overcome by delusions
of grandeur.

Dominance is its own form of frailty.

The burnt grass and rusted cars
extend forever.
There is more that binds us
than divides us.
I'm glad you're gone.

Dear Pedro Martinez

O Boston, you're filling gutters
with your October silence.

No place you'd rather be.
You must put them on your back.

The delivery's toreador flourish
Hurricane Isabel,

The pure delivery, built for its own obsolescence,
dominance is its own form of frailty.

Montreal
And on the fifth day

Dear Sandy Koufax

We threaten eternity with our monuments.
Hurricane Isabel works up the coast,
coastal flooding, property damage
Mystic waterfall, yellow hammer.
The eye of it. Bonus baby, living in the far fields
The mechanism of
The pure delivery, built for its own obsolescence.
"We drove that car as far as we could."

Dear Dontrelle Willis

Eye of the storm. Fernandomania.
Dontrelle, I believe I can confide in you:
I have not written a word in weeks.
I am occasionally afflicted by a laconic hysteria,
overcome by delusions of grandeur.

Like Hurricane Isabel,
built for its own obsolescence
We build our past to fit any myth.

Dear Greg Maddux

Frailty is its own form of dominance.
"We drove that car as far as we could."
Arbitration, there is more that binds us
Decade of futility, who could ever forget
Chicago? Pebble Beach in October?

You must put them on your back.
Two seam fastball, cutter, pitch counts,
petulance, sign of the times.

Dear Barry Zito

Yellow hammer, the hook, fish-hook,
yakker, Uncle Charlie, deuce, bender,
breaking ball, pretzel, twelve to six,
soap bubble, the snake, dropsy, lollipop,
mystic waterfall,

I don't mean to be hyperbolic.

Dear Fidel Castro

We will build our past to fit any myth.
Scouted by the Senators,
Rhapsodic as shirt sleeves.
Yellow hammer.
Yellow sickle.

History is a poor eternity.
I am thinking of the cool shaded rooms of Havana,
the opulent ruin,
Built for its own obsolescence.

Hey, Coca-Cola!
Rain in the bottom of the sixth.

Dear Gaylord Perry

What's in a name?
And if I were an umpire,
"Can you guess my weight?"

Petulance, the secret is not
what you throw
but what they think you throw.

There are one hundred million
private Halls of Fame.

Eleven enough beside you.
Low sun scud.
North star, North Carolina, Southern
California

Dear Charlie Hough

I've been thinking about you for a long time.
Were the Niekro brothers ever young
like Paul Newman?

"It's like trying to eat jello with chopsticks."
"Like trying to catch a butterfly with a pair of tweezers."
"A butterfly with hiccups."

The opulent ruin of rotation,
the pure delivery, the mechanism of
Hurricane Isabel.

Aberdeen Iron Birds, Chattanooga Lookouts, Eugene Emeralds,
Frisco Roughriders, Greensboro Bats, Hickory Crawdads,
Jupiter Hammerheads, Montgomery Biscuits, Savanna Sand-Gnats,
Wichita Wranglers, Yakima Bears.

Morandi Sequence

Arcades brick dust a rose lamp burns in the upstairs window   every-
thing I will say I have said already   still again the arcades the dust the
light to be built by the bottle the box   I will say saucer   I have said
everything   I will say

                                        *

The accumulation of transparent planes brims with ashes in a cup
reducible to rain running from the awnings of arcades   a girl carry-
ing a pitcher of water through half-dark dust stirred by the bulk of her
skirt suspends   I can still reach toward that past   saying "snarl of
sun" I opened and closed the door of a telephone booth watching the
coil redden and dim   I saw your street in a photograph   a tangle of
black thread crossed out

                                        *

Your tongue is a letter   I have not written in days   it took all day to
load the trees with silence the street with quartz   the lamp carves
a semi-circle from the wall   distance again cleaves (the mirror, etc)
light again from dark between which the dust settles uniformly   I
have been talking to you now for two days at a time   I will try not to
think about swallowing my tongue

                                        *

The past an idea veiled as an image   I have been happy for some
time who knows why   it is cold here very cold   I measure these
things in smaller and smaller increments   *perhaps we can only relate
to our own imaginings   perhaps we are only in love with our own images*
what did you take me for

                                        *

By now I'm beginning in smaller and smaller increments   the trees
load themselves with silence the arcades with dust the bottle with
light   in a semi-circle she carries an umbrella through the pitcher of
the room   as before   it must be full day now for the dust settles
so uniformly

                                        *

It's only evenings augured open after all and the quartz streets
strange lattice of light detached from space by the tremors of their
shape   objects themselves our medians or mediations   touch with
shadows the far off light on the facades facets   a rose lamp burn-
ing   everything I have said and will endeavor

Stars of Stage and Screen

Torpor issues honey
August, the color
of your hair.

Stars of stage and screen,
we are awake to the night
of Gray's Papaya,

Rain coming up.
To writ small.
To day across.

Morning-dark to raven-
der
Entangled stars, a bucket of fish.

And I felt at once quite still
in my wishes, lasting,
last.
Rush to stasis.

How blue your yellow hair.   And the landscapes of Norway.

And your house thrice torn down   but once by death.

There is shouting here all the time.   Here all the time.

Blue thistle script of an old letter,   sepia continents of stamps.

Dear past, that rushes into the dense blue   afternoons under March

and wells with all its sleeping, nascent,   blooms.

Greening the landscape   machine.

What black light   founders your words.

This ringing quiet.   Nostalgia debris in the shipyard.

In time the images will come.   The Newspaper District, Berlin 1918.

The Hanover Glass Factory Fire.   You venture out into despondent

night. Inking in puddles, in spots clinging   the billboards papered in strip

beginning to peel.   Your face shines through the architecture.

Stitching a button back on a coat,   eyes back on a reflection.

Stitching gathering.   Carving our from an hourglass.

Like the satin trim of a blanket, the spaces   (I myself) are coming apart.

On Violet Street.   On Violet Street.

North Front

The orange municipal trucks back up,
dead grass, waist-high, ruffles in the parting wind
Many years in the wish of darkness.
The parade of labor spreads salt in the new streets.
Two days indoors,
My mind is the Cotton Bowl, the Orange Bowl,
the running game of Ole Miss.
How sweet from the shower you steam
after a haircut. The New Year
is orange. Lentils the color of money.
River-boat captain, you are beautiful
by starlight –
crumbs in your wake for the birds, and for the moths,
a winter porch-light.

1
The bees are waking up.
The bees are flying slowly
in the air.
I don't want to die.

The rum interior of spring.
I have taken to the streets
in my bathrobe.
Trees are popsicles

which is filled with music as
green is vigorous – stinging
is what hurts
where your hands are.

If tears are vows
I have been disabused
all this time –
Her hair smells like a spent match.

2
The neighbor's curtains have been taken down,
and the mercury is cloud's fluorescence.

Five fingers are to the State Police
as poison to the eye.

Spectacles too are their own light.
Baseball on television.

Kansas City 8	Toronto 3
Boston 3	Baltimore 1
New York 4	Seattle 9

On the east side
the avenues unfurl in order:
Lexington, Madison, Park, Fifth.

And the sky is white
over Simone Weil tonight.

3 Epithalamium
School bus yellow my teeth
hurt. Everyone is getting ready:
the Lakers are out in six,
July is rose like the ocean,
the mountains are golden like
Susan Lucci's daytime Emmy.

It is an amber morning:
bees to their hive, rum
to their bottle, trombones
to their dusky voice.

Even the bride is playing
Pick Six. Grime on the sill,
song in my heart:

California, California,
O California, California.
California, O California,
California, California.

Stalwart and Flood Time

You're darking and coffee
the bedpost my pinion,
my stevedore. Allay always.
Offer up everything: truth

be told I'd rather
be fishing,
and so on.
Collage of startled
flight, mottled rain. Steeples

from the rising oxbow
of the Charles.

Weatherchild.

Commute

To what arrival's question
To splay in the dark of what dream
As mezzotint autumn

How we wake
into knowing
waking

Every cajole in the heart
Panoply wishes at Prince
and Broadway

Bone bruise, Ford GT, Stamford
Connecticut
in the faint diamonds of precipitation

Oxygen is to rust
as
a.) Brink to cash
b.) Raisins to grapes
c.) Laptop to lust

But on a more personal note
the loneliest girls
are always named "Hope"

Palermo

1
At night my stomach hurts.
In the dark crumbling arch
of a door a dog barks.

A drift of leaves bursts
like a bank of birds,
like the stone foal of your thought.

And we say *to see with new eyes.*
Buried in blue,
choked in the throttle of color.

This I could never spell with your hands:
the body too in revolt.

2
As one with whom I've come to live,
turbulent poplars toss in the wind –
and the leaves do fall and cut their margins

in autumn air. A peeling blue cupola
shoulders the stations of the sun.
I think at times some better than this.

The small bridge of her,
a darkening bridge opens its wheel.

3
How the seasons come unwrapped:
a rash like an orchid swells beneath my shirt.
And the bathroom tile green like morning.

[Refrain]

Now is the hour and the breath.
Now the station stops flit by and their graffiti.

Ocean Park

Sparse forested continuously
lakes swift its long coastline.
Confetti islands sea sea.

Government railroads patchwork
the constitution. Television
aerials the hilly regions.

The future makes me sad.
To think of glaciers,
rocks, rocky beaches,
can usually understand each other.

Telephones automobiles and television
sets. Settled slope gently
eastward unpopulated, modern and efficient.

Suicide trees their larkspur.
Your hair slowly fills the drain.

Southern plains most
courts. Ancient urban tribes
Baltic provinces diminishing
differences.

Boundaries inner north.
Enterprise and industry.
Widows annual folktales,

country homes, children attend
beaches during the summer
the sun shines 24 hours a day.

How blithe and wonder.
Service and industry, the mine's
winds are missionary work.

People settled farther north
as improved. Old Caspian,
most westward encouraged
islands, struggles, rout.

Your windlass fertile mid-February.
Boy, subway,
azalea. Farmlands and forests
of beechwood. Miles.

Retire suns of wonder,
wood pulp crowns in a field.
Most are facts their gloss.

Urgent and utmost. To tease
blooms from a frivolous film.
Arial farmlands spare horizons,
horizons most.

Square blue unpopulated.
Walks on the seashore
strike Prussian. Light-colored
and simple –

Small glaciers, in part,
heart. Ships carry good
coastal towns.
The east then fell as dispatched
expeditions settled vaguely
rain beneath emotions.

Fjords cross electric
in the storms. The union
of temperatures flat
an expanse. Tissue of snow,
climate, winds, network, weld.

Porches dutch in evening's awning.

Patina royal in pattern light.
Sand in the tire tracks, dull bronzed
of gauze let
Saltwater honor
native portraits.

Rope colored I've been sick.
Winter sun slugs it out.
Rainfall influenced architects
develop privately.

Foreign foreign your squares
and tangles. Board-feet, Drano,
is a measure of

Followers mainland
sheets of farms and salt

Marsh.

Revolt encouraged warmer, lower
unions. Snow-capped and
There are problems

for which there are no solutions.
There are some problems for which
there are no solutions.

As those, who well cared for,
Does not point toward happiness or
an afterlife.

Long the day's sandy approach.

Flowers in December

Steam from the laundry room at street level
fills the air with spring, and a shadow –
Empty park on Thursday afternoon
in December.
Sports radio.
Indeed, strangers are frightening.
Billeted as such.

A shadow of warmth
I am listening to a recording
of Mazzy Star singing "Flowers in December".
Dizzy in the mix
from cold to sleet to snow to rain
Jet Blue, I'll be the one
to undress you.

The Novice

Now the city's body is an ark: the river
bends back on itself.

Water, stained with mercury, climbs the gutters.
The red morning sky vaguely patriotic.

I have learned to resemble myself: colors
mixed with milk. On the night-stand

a glass of water grows small white spots.
It rained deeply.

Between streetlights, beneath an arch I cast two
shadows or, 'how I began to fall in love'.

An arm across her larynx: the fingers, fan-like,
birds in flight, they stutter, misspelling her name.

It is dark in the funnel of the horizon.
Not stars, not stars appear.

Confetti

Till the lapse.
Brocade too
Fingers in the window

How small
you appear
in the distance

The time-lapse suns
on adolescent stems
Intermittently for instance
is cold outside

And we imagine
we see
in the season itself
the signs of the season's
demise,

window-softly

Dear Fugue, Dear Figment

The Pier

Field tufted with pilings,   sea under fallen snow,

promise of a horizon.   One thing and one thing , divisions,

latitudes. Move into the first   browns of spring,

imagine suddenly a depth.   No longer, no longer, nor buoyed

by cupped hands. It is not fog that obscures

the view, but indistinguishable mediums: the diffuse sky

hunched or vague   tides drawn and sunk.

Sheaves of hair drizzle from a sieve.   *Here is a sentence*

in which she does not appear.   Have I said "hull".

A salt stream runs opposite the train tracks,   an anchor rusts

like an abandoned   plow. Arms scatter their hands dismissive

from a supposed center. This is March   coming up like a sun.

The shutter whirrs.   An anchor rusts like a kedge.

Field under fallen snow,   sea spiked with pilings.

Here, the hollow of a hand   sieves the spokes of a stream. Latitude

seeks its circumference,   I am counting one thing and one thing.

I am listing. The broken slats   of the pier-head. Parallels,

the disillusion of perspective. Think: one year has passed and it's still

March, mid-month,   forsythia coming up like kedge.

But that we could all stand,   in such a way, accidentally.

The future has arrived   and it is not unbearable,

as promised.

The overpass silvers   its crescent of river, late-winter.

The eye seeks itself: *I am known,*   spelled none.

Engine Marchember

Engine Marchember,
wild in the sleeves
of the park. Ghostly appendages
Unprovoked
teapot, tipping point –
moment of everyday death.

Sun with the teeth
of a gear. Crocus rupture
Spring
hauls itself through the thaw of its inheritance.
Once there was no longer
door closed, locks changed.

The Mingulay Boat Song

Abrupt and foxglove. The wind scales back.
Dragonflies sprout from bow
to gunnel; bluebottles pour from every seam.

The body pierced by a small hole,
or the lampshade, invents you.
Speaking of the Hebrides,

a schooner like a dark smudge on a dark
sea hauls to windward.
The way you wring the ropes of your hair.

The way a deserted village spoils
on its hinges. The way sheep
graze among the cobblestones.

A larynx stems its chords.
Coax, wrack and sigh, threshing of sun –
And the door, to the wind, blown in.

Four Portraits of Kira Sleeping

a simple blue / unphrased
— BASIL BUNTING, ODES

1
Patchwork bulk of sea-script.
Needlepoint night.
The last breath I hear
is always out
And the second hand

2
The courtyard
more lovely
than a fluorescent sconce.

A tremble
runs the length
of your body.

It is 2 am so why am I still
I will row I
hear oars

I will row this boat
toward the shores of
And I hear

you are mumbling
Gently toward you.

3
A little tumult in
unbuttoned calligraphy

4
You're a hurricane
in hotpants I
a coastal trailer-park.

Batting Cleanup for the Los Angeles Dodgers

That same old feeling,
a pop song.
Sky choral.
Difficult what slow
it is. I grind
my teeth in my sleep.

It is wrong
to want to punt
the child that wails
in the night. I remind
myself, it is wrong
to want

We are out of doors
goes the sales pitch
for spring
like the Home Depot.

Soft blue trees stain
the edges of the afternoon.

Conviction Want

Each day is everything
like the rest
By threes undoes us.

Thrush eve's thunder,
surf of traffic from the west
Side Highway.

Seashore machine
By sevens, by threes.
The high metallic whine

of katydids or a neighbor's
air conditioner.
This hammer heart

Snow white, bone white,
cloud white, stone white
Empathy is divisive.

Sandy Hook

Sandy Hook, there are lilacs and
detergent. Equations drawn in the sand.
This is the how do you live.
Soulful senorita, sweet-smelling as a lilac
tattoo. I've never been as far as the Jersey Shore
either. But autumning's fast car,
the street slicked with fallen leaves –
sirens dopple from the highway.

Pine Sol, Oleander, The Gold Coast –
there is a bucket in my chest,
dear Liza, dear Liza
who will fill it?
Flies at the screen are

Hurricane in Steerage

Like a rose from a pencil sharpener
the sun wound up sewing
after [illegible]

desolate thunderclaps and
from a payphone on Pearl Street,
in the silo nesting swallows.

The Endurance, The Bounty, The Blue Balls,
The Jolly Roger—
built properties of falling,
water, oxygen, parasols and pennants.

Music up the aviary,
the bilge, under emergency
lights.

Now I will have my say:
"Sun will you dry the deck chairs?
my towel?"

Patience pretty
vacant blue.
Castors all.

Fluorescent Flowers

There are few who sleep as I do
in the Metropolitan Museum.

Kinoko, you and I
standing on the Bow Bridge
dressed in the purple of nightfall.

Kinoko, you and I
shaving our legs before the swim-meet.

Fluorescence floral –
It has begun to February

in your eyes.

The first calligraphic pen-stroke
revealed the error of my ways.

Drunk, Theraflu, passing through
the pale blue snow of television.